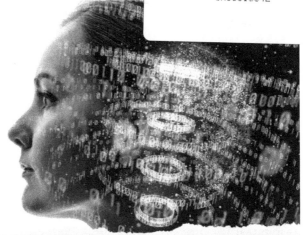

Narrative Nexus: The AI Dilemma in Fiction

Should AI Replace Fictional Writers?

B Alan Bourgeois

B Alan Bourgeois

Narrative Nexus: The AI Dilemma in Fiction

© B Alan Bourgeois 2023

ISBN#9781088285930

Publisher: Bourgeois Media & Consulting (BourgeoisMedia.com)

BOURGEOIS
MEDIA & CONSULTING

Introduction

Should AI replace Fictional Writers, and if so, why? Is the question we proposed and wanted to know what AI would say. The following response will be detailed in the chapters that follow.

The question of whether AI should replace fictional writers is a complex and debated topic that involves various perspectives. Here are some arguments both in favor and against the idea:

Arguments in Favor of AI Replacing Fictional Writers:

1. **Efficiency and Output:** AI can generate content at an incredibly fast rate. This could lead to a higher volume of creative works being produced, satisfying the demand for more content.
2. **Exploration of New Ideas:** AI algorithms can analyze vast amounts of data and generate unique combinations of ideas that human writers might not have thought of, leading to innovative and unexpected storylines.
3. **Accessibility:** AI-generated content can be tailored to various audiences, languages, and genres, making literature more accessible to a global audience.
4. **Experimentation:** AI can be used as a tool for writers to experiment with different styles, genres, and narrative structures. It can provide suggestions that challenge conventional storytelling norms.

Arguments Against AI Replacing Fictional Writers:

1. **Creativity and Emotional Depth:** Human writers bring their unique experiences, emotions, and perspectives to their

work, leading to a depth of creativity and emotional resonance that AI might struggle to replicate.

2. **Artistic Expression:** Writing is not just about conveying information; it's also a form of artistic expression. Human writers infuse their work with their individuality, which can't be easily replicated by AI.

3. **Human Connection:** Readers often connect with authors on a personal level through their work. The authenticity of a human-authored piece can create a deeper emotional bond between the writer and the audience.

4. **Ethical and Social Concerns:** AI-generated content raises questions about intellectual property, originality, and cultural significance. Plagiarism and copyright infringement could become more challenging to address.

5. **Uniqueness and Originality:** AI generates content based on existing data, which might limit its ability to create truly unique and original stories. Human writers draw inspiration from a wide range of sources and experiences.

6. **Quality and Cohesion:** While AI can generate text, it might struggle with maintaining consistent quality, coherent narrative arcs, and nuanced character development that human writers excel at.

In conclusion, while AI has the potential to assist writers in various ways, fully replacing human fiction writers remains a contentious issue. AI-generated content might excel in certain aspects, such as generating ideas and experimenting with styles, but it might struggle to replicate the depth, emotion, and authenticity that human writers bring to their work. A more likely scenario is that AI will be used as a tool to augment and complement human creativity rather than completely replace it.

Contents

Part 1
Arguments in Favor of AI Replacing Fictional Writers

1
Efficiency and Output

AI can generate content at an incredibly fast rate. This could lead to a higher volume of creative works being produced, satisfying the demand for more content.

One of the primary advantages of using AI to replace fictional writers is the significant increase in efficiency and output that AI systems can achieve. AI algorithms, particularly those based on neural networks like GPT-3, have the capacity to generate text at a rapid pace. This ability has several implications that support the idea of AI replacing fictional writers:

1. **Rapid Content Creation:** AI algorithms can produce large amounts of text in a short period of time. This means that authors who are under pressure to meet deadlines or who want to publish content quickly can benefit from AI-generated drafts.
2. **Meeting High Demand:** The global demand for various forms of content, including books, articles, short stories, and more, is substantial. AI-generated content can help meet this demand by producing a higher volume of material than human writers alone.
3. **Variety of Genres and Styles:** AI can generate content in various genres, styles, and tones. This versatility can cater to a wide range of audience preferences and interests, expanding the availability of content across different niches.
4. **Experimentation and Iteration:** AI can quickly generate multiple versions of a story or explore different narrative paths. This enables authors and publishers to experiment with ideas and iterate on concepts rapidly.

5. **Serialized Content:** For platforms that rely on serialized content delivery, such as web novels or interactive storytelling apps, AI can provide a consistent stream of new content to keep audiences engaged.
6. **Resource Optimization:** While AI can generate initial drafts, human writers can then focus on refining and editing the content. This division of labor can optimize the use of human resources and creativity.
7. **Supporting Collaborative Work:** AI-generated content can serve as a starting point for collaboration between AI systems and human writers. This can enhance the creative process by providing a foundation that writers can build upon.
8. **Language and Translation:** AI-generated content can be translated into multiple languages quickly, expanding the reach of a story to a global audience.

While the efficiency and high output of AI-generated content are notable advantages, it's important to consider that this efficiency doesn't necessarily guarantee the same level of creativity, emotional depth, and authenticity that human writers bring to their work. The challenge lies in finding a balance between utilizing AI's capabilities for rapid content creation while also preserving the unique qualities that make human-authored fiction impactful and meaningful.

2
Exploration of New Ideas

AI algorithms can analyze vast amounts of data and generate unique combinations of ideas that human writers might not have thought of, leading to innovative and unexpected storylines.

One of the intriguing aspects of AI in the context of fiction writing is its potential to push the boundaries of creativity by exploring new and unconventional ideas. This argument suggests that AI can enhance the creative process by introducing fresh perspectives and imaginative concepts that might not have emerged from human writers alone. Here's a detailed explanation of this argument:

1. **Data Analysis and Pattern Recognition:** AI systems are capable of analyzing and processing enormous amounts of data from various sources, such as literature, historical texts, scientific articles, and more. Through this analysis, AI can identify patterns, trends, and connections that might be overlooked by human writers.
2. **Cross-Disciplinary Inspiration:** AI algorithms can draw inspiration from a wide range of disciplines and genres. By synthesizing information from fields as diverse as astronomy, psychology, art history, and folklore, AI can create stories that incorporate unique elements from different domains.
3. **Serendipitous Connections:** AI's ability to process data at scale can lead to serendipitous discoveries. It might link seemingly unrelated ideas, leading to innovative and surprising storylines that human writers might not have envisioned.

4. **Breaking Conventional Norms:** AI is not bound by traditional storytelling conventions or preconceived notions. This freedom can result in narratives that challenge established norms and experiment with unconventional structures, pacing, and character arcs.
5. **Unbiased Idea Generation:** Unlike humans, AI doesn't have inherent biases, preferences, or emotional attachments. This neutrality can lead to the exploration of ideas that might be outside a human writer's comfort zone or worldview.
6. **Assisting Writer's Block:** AI-generated prompts and ideas can help writers overcome creative blocks. Writers can use AI-generated concepts as starting points to build upon and develop their stories.
7. **Promoting Innovation:** AI-generated storylines can introduce novel concepts to the literary landscape, sparking discussions and encouraging other writers to think outside the box.
8. **Enhancing Creativity:** Human writers can collaborate with AI as a source of inspiration. AI-generated prompts can ignite creative thinking and encourage writers to expand their creative horizons.

However, it's important to note that while AI can introduce innovative ideas, the execution of these ideas into compelling narratives often requires the touch of human creativity, emotional depth, and understanding of human psychology. Additionally, AI-generated content might lack the emotional resonance and personal connections that human authors bring to their work. Therefore, the role of AI in introducing new ideas should be seen as a tool to complement and inspire human writers rather than to completely replace them.

3
Accessibility

AI-generated content can be tailored to various audiences, languages, and genres, making literature more accessible to a global audience.

The accessibility argument emphasizes the potential of AI to democratize literature and make it available to a wider range of people around the world. AI's capacity to produce content that suits different languages, cultures, and preferences can contribute to making literature more inclusive and expansive. Here's a detailed explanation of this argument:

1. **Multilingual Content:** AI's language translation capabilities can break down language barriers by enabling stories to be quickly translated into multiple languages. This ensures that literary works are accessible to non-native speakers and readers from diverse linguistic backgrounds.
2. **Global Reach:** AI-generated content can span various cultural contexts and cater to readers with different cultural references and preferences. This can create a richer literary landscape that encompasses stories from various parts of the world.
3. **Genre and Niche Exploration:** AI's ability to generate content in various genres and niches means that it can cater to specific reader interests that might not be well-served by traditional publishing. This opens up opportunities for niche literature to gain wider recognition.
4. **Tailored Reading Levels:** AI can adapt the complexity and vocabulary of its content based on the intended audience's

reading level, making literature more accessible to different age groups and literacy levels.

5. **Personalization:** AI-generated content can be personalized based on individual preferences, delivering stories that resonate with readers on a more personal level. This can lead to more engaging reading experiences.

6. **Representation and Diversity:** AI can help amplify underrepresented voices and stories. By generating content that reflects a broader range of experiences, cultures, and perspectives, AI can contribute to greater diversity in literature.

7. **Cultural Exchange:** AI-generated content that draws inspiration from various cultures can facilitate cultural exchange and understanding, promoting empathy and connection among readers from different backgrounds.

8. **Reviving Classic Works:** AI can be used to modernize and adapt classic literary works, making them more accessible to contemporary readers while preserving their original essence.

9. **Rapid Response to Demand:** In rapidly evolving situations or emerging trends, AI-generated content can quickly provide relevant stories that address current events or popular topics.

While AI's ability to create accessible content is compelling, it's important to recognize that cultural nuances, emotional depth, and authenticity might be lost in the process of automated content generation. Human writers often infuse their works with a deep understanding of the human condition, emotions, and societal intricacies that AI might not fully grasp. Therefore, while AI can enhance accessibility, the role of human writers in crafting stories with genuine emotional resonance remains indispensable.

4
Experimentation

AI can be used as a tool for writers to experiment with different styles, genres, and narrative structures. It can provide suggestions that challenge conventional storytelling norms.

The experimentation argument highlights how AI technology can function as a creative collaborator, helping human writers explore new avenues of storytelling and break away from traditional norms. By suggesting innovative ideas and unconventional approaches, AI can inspire writers to push the boundaries of their craft. Here's a detailed explanation of this argument:

1. **Creative Prompting:** AI-generated prompts and ideas can act as catalysts for writers' creativity. These prompts might introduce concepts or scenarios that writers might not have considered, sparking fresh creative thinking.
2. **Genre Fusion:** AI can suggest combinations of genres that might lead to unique and exciting cross-genre stories. This can result in refreshing narratives that captivate readers with unexpected blends.
3. **Narrative Structures:** AI can propose alternative narrative structures, timelines, and perspectives that challenge the traditional linear storytelling format. This experimentation can create engaging and dynamic reading experiences.
4. **Character Development:** AI can provide insights into character personalities, motivations, and interactions that human writers might not have initially imagined. This can lead to more complex and well-rounded characters.
5. **World-Building:** AI can contribute to the creation of imaginative and intricate fictional worlds by suggesting

details, cultures, histories, and rules that enrich the setting of a story.

6. **Incorporating New Media:** As storytelling evolves to include various media formats, AI can assist in incorporating elements like interactive elements, multimedia, and branching narratives.
7. **Breaking Stereotypes:** AI-generated content can challenge stereotypes and biases by suggesting unconventional character traits, relationships, and story arcs that go against common tropes.
8. **Enhancing Writer's Skill Set:** Writers can learn from AI-generated suggestions and apply new techniques to their work, expanding their repertoire of skills and approaches.
9. **Subverting Expectations:** AI-generated ideas can introduce plot twists and unexpected outcomes, subverting reader expectations and leading to more engaging narratives.
10. **Iterative Process:** Writers can collaborate with AI in an iterative process, refining and evolving AI-generated concepts to align with their creative vision.

While AI's experimentation capabilities offer exciting possibilities, it's essential to recognize that the essence of creative storytelling often comes from the human experience, emotions, and unique perspectives that human writers bring to their work. AI can contribute to experimentation, but the ability to weave these experimental elements into a coherent, emotionally resonant, and relatable narrative remains a distinct human skill that cannot be fully replicated by technology alone. Therefore, the interaction between AI and human creativity can lead to dynamic and innovative storytelling while maintaining the depth that human authors contribute.

Part 2
Arguments Against AI Replacing Fictional Writers

1
Creativity and Emotional Depth

Human writers bring their unique experiences, emotions, and perspectives to their work, leading to a depth of creativity and emotional resonance that AI might struggle to replicate.

This argument underscores the deeply personal and human elements that contribute to the richness of fictional storytelling. It emphasizes that human writers' capacity to infuse their work with their emotions, life experiences, and distinctive viewpoints results in a level of creativity and emotional depth that might be challenging for AI to emulate. Here's a detailed explanation of this argument:

1. **Emotional Authenticity:** Human writers draw from their own emotions, memories, and personal experiences to imbue their characters and narratives with authentic feelings. Readers often connect with these emotions on a profound level, creating a lasting impact.
2. **Empathy and Understanding:** Human writers have the ability to deeply understand and portray a wide range of emotions and complex human experiences. They can accurately depict the subtleties of love, grief, joy, and other intricate emotions that resonate with readers.
3. **Cultural and Contextual Sensitivity:** Writers' cultural backgrounds and life experiences inform their perspectives on societal issues, relationships, and more. This enables them to create stories that resonate with specific cultures or address nuanced social themes.
4. **Uniqueness of Voice:** Each writer has a unique voice and style that is shaped by their personality, beliefs, and individual writing journey. This uniqueness contributes to a

diverse literary landscape and offers readers a variety of perspectives.

5. **Narrative Insight:** Human writers often draw on their observations of human behavior and psychology, resulting in characters and stories that reflect the complexities of human interactions and motivations.

6. **Vulnerability and Honesty:** Writers' willingness to share personal vulnerabilities and truths can result in deeply moving and relatable narratives that evoke strong emotional responses from readers.

7. **Originality and Innovation:** Human creativity extends beyond generating ideas; it involves crafting original plots, character developments, and narrative twists that challenge conventional norms and expectations.

8. **Adaptation and Evolution:** Human writers adapt to evolving cultural, social, and technological landscapes, infusing their stories with contemporary relevance and resonating with modern audiences.

9. **Exploration of the Human Condition:** Through their writing, human authors explore philosophical questions, existential dilemmas, and the essence of what it means to be human. This depth adds philosophical and intellectual dimensions to their work.

While AI can assist in various aspects of the creative process, such as generating ideas and assisting with certain writing tasks, replicating the emotional depth, unique voice, and personal connection that human writers bring to their stories remains a significant challenge. AI's lack of personal experiences, emotions, and the capacity for genuine vulnerability can limit its ability to evoke the same range of emotions and create stories that deeply resonate with readers. The collaboration between AI and human writers holds potential for innovative storytelling, but the qualities that make human-authored fiction truly exceptional are likely to endure.

2

Artistic Expression

Writing is not just about conveying information; it's also a form of artistic expression. Human writers infuse their work with their individuality, which can't be easily replicated by AI.

The argument of artistic expression underscores the unique and irreplaceable contribution that human writers make to the world of literature. Beyond the mere conveyance of information, writing is an art form that allows individuals to communicate their thoughts, emotions, and perspectives in a deeply personal and creative manner. Here's a detailed explanation of this argument:

1. **Subjectivity and Interpretation:** Artistic expression is inherently subjective and often open to interpretation. Human writers weave their own thoughts, emotions, and beliefs into their narratives, creating layers of meaning that invite readers to engage with the text on multiple levels.
2. **Voice and Style:** Every writer has a distinct voice and style that is shaped by their life experiences, cultural background, personality, and personal growth. This uniqueness contributes to a diverse literary landscape where each author's work stands out.
3. **Nuanced Themes and Messages:** Human writers craft narratives that explore complex themes, moral dilemmas, and philosophical questions. These nuanced explorations reflect the author's intellectual depth and perspective, offering readers a deeper understanding of the human condition.
4. **Metaphor and Symbolism:** Skilled writers use metaphor, symbolism, and literary devices to convey abstract concepts, emotions, and ideas. These artistic elements add layers of

depth to the text, allowing readers to engage with multi-dimensional narratives.

5. **Emotional Resonance:** The emotional impact of a story often comes from the personal investment of the writer. Human writers infuse their characters and events with emotional authenticity, leading to genuine connections with readers.

6. **Creative Interpretation of Reality:** Writers reimagine reality through their creativity, presenting familiar scenarios in fresh and imaginative ways. This perspective can challenge societal norms, provoke thought, and inspire change.

7. **Experimental Approaches:** Human writers push the boundaries of narrative structures, linguistic experimentation, and storytelling techniques. This experimentation stems from the desire to innovate and explore new creative frontiers.

8. **Cultural Significance:** Throughout history, literature has been a reflection of cultural, social, and political contexts. Human writers contribute to the cultural legacy by addressing contemporary issues through their artistic lens.

9. **Personal Catharsis:** Writing serves as a cathartic outlet for human experiences, allowing writers to process emotions, confront personal demons, and share their journeys with others.

While AI can assist in generating content, its limitations lie in its inability to truly understand the depths of human emotion, the intricacies of personal experiences, and the nuances of artistic expression. AI may mimic patterns and structures found in existing texts, but the genuine creativity, authenticity, and individuality that human writers bring to their work remain unparalleled. The interplay between AI's capabilities and human creativity can lead to exciting possibilities, but it's the human touch that preserves the soul of literary art.

3
Human Connection

Readers often connect with authors on a personal level through their work. The authenticity of a human-authored piece can create a deeper emotional bond between the writer and the audience.

The argument regarding human connection underscores the emotional resonance that exists between writers and their readers. It highlights the unique ability of human writers to forge a genuine connection with their audience through their authenticity, relatability, and shared human experiences. Here's a detailed explanation of this argument:

1. **Empathy and Shared Experiences:** Human writers draw from their own lives, emotions, and struggles to create characters and narratives that resonate with readers' own experiences. This shared emotional journey allows readers to connect on a profound level.
2. **Relatability:** Readers often find comfort and solace in knowing that they are not alone in their thoughts and feelings. Human writers' personal touch and relatable narratives create a sense of camaraderie and understanding.
3. **Cultural and Social Context:** Human writers infuse their work with cultural nuances, societal observations, and personal reflections that resonate with readers' own cultural backgrounds and life contexts.
4. **Authorial Intent:** Understanding an author's background, motivations, and intentions can deepen readers' appreciation of a work. The human touch behind the narrative choices adds layers of meaning that AI-generated content might lack.

5. **Reader Engagement:** Personal insights, anecdotes, and authorial commentary provide readers with insights into the creative process and the motivations behind the story. This engagement enhances the reading experience.
6. **Literary Conversations:** Readers often engage in discussions, analysis, and interpretations of an author's work. The author's unique perspective contributes to these conversations and enhances the overall literary discourse.
7. **Influence on Identity:** Some readers develop a strong connection with certain authors, and the themes explored in their work might influence readers' personal development, beliefs, and identity.
8. **Reader-Writer Relationship:** Over time, readers can develop a sense of loyalty and attachment to their favorite authors. This relationship adds an emotional dimension to the act of reading.
9. **Human Emotion and Vulnerability:** Human writers openly express vulnerability, fear, love, and other emotions in their work, creating an emotional bridge that readers can cross to connect with the story's themes.
10. **Literature as a Reflection of Humanity:** Literature is a mirror that reflects the human experience. Human writers infuse their work with authenticity, making it easier for readers to see themselves in the stories.

While AI-generated content can offer efficiency and innovative ideas, it might lack the deeply personal touch that human writers provide. The authenticity, vulnerability, and relatability that human authors bring to their work create a bond between writer and reader that goes beyond the words on the page. This connection is rooted in shared humanity and emotions, making the presence of human writers an essential part of the literary landscape.

4
Ethical and Social Concerns

AI-generated content raises questions about intellectual property, originality, and cultural significance. Plagiarism and copyright infringement could become more challenging to address.

The argument concerning ethical and social concerns delves into the potential complications that arise from using AI-generated content in place of human-authored fiction. It highlights the intricate web of intellectual property, creativity, and cultural sensitivities that can be disrupted by AI's ability to produce content. Here's a detailed explanation of this argument:

1. **Intellectual Property and Ownership:** AI-generated content blurs the lines of ownership and authorship. While humans input the initial programming, the AI's role in generating content challenges traditional notions of creative ownership.
2. **Originality and Creative Process:** Human authors invest their time, emotions, and thought processes into crafting original stories. AI-generated content, although it may combine existing elements, raises questions about the authenticity of the creative process.
3. **Plagiarism and Copyright:** The sheer volume of data AI processes increases the likelihood of inadvertently producing content similar to existing works. This could lead to unintentional plagiarism or accusations of copyright infringement.
4. **Cultural Appropriation:** AI might lack the understanding to navigate sensitive cultural contexts, potentially producing content that appropriates or misrepresents cultural elements, leading to backlash.

5. **Cultural Significance:** Literature often holds cultural and historical significance. AI-generated stories might not accurately capture these nuances, undermining the cultural value of literature.
6. **Lack of Intention and Consciousness:** AI lacks intentionality and consciousness. This raises concerns about the depth of meaning in the content it generates and whether it can truly reflect the complex human experience.
7. **Socioeconomic Implications:** If AI-generated content becomes prevalent, professional writers might face diminished opportunities and income, impacting the livelihoods of those in the creative industry.
8. **Loss of Craftsmanship:** The art of writing involves honing one's craft, cultivating a unique voice, and developing narrative skills over time. AI's role in generating content could undermine the craftsmanship of storytelling.
9. **Long-Term Artistic Development:** A significant part of an author's growth comes from struggling with creativity, learning from failures, and refining one's skills. Relying solely on AI-generated content might hinder this development.
10. **Diminished Cultural Diversity:** AI's reliance on existing data might favor mainstream themes and perspectives, leading to a homogenization of literature and marginalizing diverse voices.

The ethical and social implications of AI-generated content extend beyond the act of writing itself. They touch on matters of creative integrity, cultural respect, and the preservation of the artistic and literary traditions that have shaped societies for centuries. While AI has the potential to aid writers, the nuances and ethical considerations of the creative process underscore the continued importance of human writers in safeguarding the authenticity and value of literature.

5
Uniqueness and Originality

AI generates content based on existing data, which might limit its ability to create truly unique and original stories. Human writers draw inspiration from a wide range of sources and experiences.

The argument regarding uniqueness and originality underscores the concern that AI-generated content might lack the genuine novelty and creativity that come from human writers' ability to draw inspiration from diverse sources and experiences. It emphasizes the distinctiveness and multi-faceted nature of human creativity that contributes to the richness of literature. Here's a detailed explanation of this argument:

1. **Source of Inspiration:** Human writers draw from a vast array of experiences, emotions, memories, and interactions that inform their narratives. These individual experiences contribute to the uniqueness of their storytelling.
2. **Cognitive Imagination:** Humans have the ability to imagine beyond existing data and experiences. They can synthesize seemingly unrelated concepts to create innovative and fresh storylines.
3. **Exploration of the Unknown:** AI relies on patterns in data it has already processed. Human writers, on the other hand, are driven by curiosity to explore the unknown and delve into uncharted territory.
4. **Subconscious Creativity:** Human creativity often arises from the subconscious mind, combining fragments of thoughts and experiences that might not be explicitly recorded in existing data.
5. **Cross-Disciplinary Influence:** Human authors often draw inspiration from fields outside of literature, such as science,

history, music, and art. This cross-disciplinary influence adds depth and complexity to their narratives.

6. **Personal Interpretation:** Human writers interpret their experiences and observations in unique ways. This personal interpretation enriches their stories with layers of meaning that AI might struggle to replicate.
7. **Innovation Beyond Patterns:** While AI identifies patterns in existing data, it might miss the potential for breakthroughs that result from defying patterns and introducing entirely new ideas.
8. **Transcending Limitations:** Human writers have the capacity to transcend their own limitations and create narratives that go beyond their personal experiences, expanding the boundaries of imagination.
9. **Cultural Synthesis:** Human creativity can result in narratives that synthesize cultural elements, historical contexts, and contemporary issues, producing a narrative tapestry that reflects a wide spectrum of influences.
10. **Evolving Inspiration:** Human writers evolve over time, drawing inspiration from changes in their personal lives and the world around them. This evolution is not solely based on existing data.

While AI-generated content can assist writers by offering suggestions and generating ideas, the inherently human qualities of imagination, curiosity, and the ability to transcend established patterns are central to the creation of original and exceptional stories. These qualities ensure that literature continues to evolve, innovate, and remain a reflection of the boundless potential of human creativity

6
Quality and Cohesion

While AI can generate text, it might struggle with maintaining consistent quality, coherent narrative arcs, and nuanced character development that human writers excel at.

The argument against AI replacing fictional writers emphasizes the intricate craftsmanship that human writers bring to storytelling, encompassing elements like quality, coherence, and character development that AI-generated content might struggle to replicate. Here's a detailed explanation of this argument:

1. **Consistent Quality:** Human writers possess the ability to maintain a consistent level of quality throughout a story, ensuring that each sentence, paragraph, and chapter contributes to the overall narrative in a meaningful way. AI-generated content may lack the discernment needed to achieve this level of consistency.
2. **Coherent Narrative Arcs:** Creating a compelling narrative requires more than just stringing together words. Human writers craft narrative arcs that build tension, reach climaxes, and provide satisfying resolutions. These arcs require a deep understanding of story structure and pacing that AI might struggle to achieve.
3. **Character Depth and Development:** Characters are the heart of any story, and human writers excel at imbuing them with depth, emotions, and growth. Human writers create characters with distinct personalities, motivations, and arcs that readers can emotionally invest in.
4. **Subtext and Nuance:** Skilled human writers layer their stories with subtext, symbolism, and thematic depth that engage readers on multiple levels. These nuanced elements

contribute to the richness of the narrative and require a deep understanding of human emotions and psychology.

5. **Emotional Resonance:** Human writers tap into their own experiences and emotions to infuse their stories with authenticity and emotional resonance. Readers connect with characters and themes on a personal level due to the genuine emotions conveyed in the writing.
6. **Creative Problem-Solving:** Storytelling often involves creative problem-solving to overcome narrative challenges. Human writers adapt and adjust their plots, characters, and settings based on the evolving needs of the story.
7. **Unique Narrative Voices:** Each writer has a unique narrative voice and style. This individuality contributes to the diversity of storytelling and offers readers a variety of perspectives and experiences.
8. **Complexity of Human Experience:** Fictional writing delves into the complex tapestry of human emotions, relationships, and experiences. Human writers can convey the nuances of these aspects in ways that resonate deeply with readers.
9. **Artistic Intuition:** Writers make intuitive decisions during the creative process that stem from their artistic instincts and expertise. These decisions contribute to the flow, rhythm, and overall aesthetic of the narrative.
10. **Reader Engagement:** Human writers can anticipate reader reactions, strategically reveal information, and employ cliffhangers to keep readers engaged and invested in the story.

While AI can generate text based on patterns in existing data, it may struggle to replicate the artistry, intuition, and emotional depth that human writers infuse into their stories. Fictional writing is a craft that encompasses more than the sum of its words; it involves shaping immersive worlds, crafting relatable characters, and eliciting emotional responses from readers. The collaborative approach of combining AI tools with human creativity holds the potential to create rich and compelling narratives that resonate deeply with audiences.

B Alan Bourgeois

About the Author

B Alan Bourgeois began his writing career at the age of 12, writing screenplays for the Adam-12 show. Despite not submitting them for review, this experience sparked his passion for writing. However, he followed the advice of his generation and pursued higher education to secure a stable job. It wasn't until 1989, after taking a writing class at a community college, that Bourgeois wrote a short story that was published. Since then, he has written over 48 short stories and published more than 10 books, including the award-winning spiritual thriller "Extinguishing the Light."

Bourgeois has become a champion for authors and founded the Texas Authors Association in 2011 to help Texas authors better market and sell their books. This led to the creation of the Texas Authors Institute of History, Inc., and the first online museum of its kind, the Texas Authors Institute. He also created several short story contests and fundraising programs for Texas students and consolidated small-town book festivals into the Lone Star Festival, promoting Texas authors, musicians, artists, and filmmakers. In 2016, he founded the Authors Marketing Event and added a Certification program in 2017, allowing attendees to gain accreditation for their hard work in learning book marketing. His recent focus has been on assisting authors of all levels to become successful Authorpreneurs through the Authors School of Business, which offers programs to help grow their careers. He is currently working with NFTs for authors to help them increase their income channels.

Top Ten Book Series and Other Books by the Author

Available at Your Favorite Bookstore

B Alan Bourgeois

100+ Questions a Writer/Author Should Ask

Looking to take your writing career to the next level? Look no further than "100+ Questions a Writer/Author Should Ask"! With over 100 questions curated by Award-Winning Author & Speaker B Alan Bourgeois, the founder and CEO of the Authors School of Business, this book is a must-have for any aspiring or established writer. Bourgeois, a seasoned publisher, author advocate, and educator, brings his wealth of experience to the table to help you better understand the publishing world and succeed in your career. Don't miss out on this valuable resource.

Top Ten Mistakes Authors Make when Creating a Book Cover

Your book cover is your first impression. Don't let a lackluster design hold you back. "Top Ten Mistakes Authors Make When Creating a Book Cover" is your comprehensive guide to avoid common pitfalls and create a cover that truly represents your work. Discover practical tips on how to choose the right colors, fonts, and design, and avoid using low-quality images and cluttered layouts. With real-world examples and expert advice, this book will help you create a cover that grabs readers' attention and leads to more sales.

Don't let a poorly designed book cover hold you back from success. Whether you're self-publishing or working with a traditional publisher, "Top Ten Mistakes Authors Make When Creating a Book Cover" is a must-read. Order your copy today and take your book to the next level!

B Alan Bourgeois

Top Ten Things to Consider for a Great Sales Pitch

Are you struggling to create a sales pitch that really resonates with your audience? Look no further than "Top Ten Things to Consider for a Great Sales Pitch"! This ultimate guide will take you through the ten most important steps to creating a sales pitch that will grab your target audience's attention and convince them to buy your book.

Learn how to identify your target audience and highlight the unique value of your book, using emotional language to connect with readers on a personal level. Be concise and to the point, and practice your pitch until you can deliver it smoothly and confidently. Incorporate social proof and visuals to make your pitch more compelling, and tailor it to the specific interests and needs of your audience.

Above all, be authentic and genuine. With the help of "Top Ten Things to Consider for a Great Sales Pitch", you'll be able to create a sales pitch that not only sells your book, but also connects with your audience and builds a loyal fan base. Don't miss out on this essential resource for any author looking to take their sales pitch to the next level!

Top Ten Publishing Issues Authors Deal With

TOP TEN
PUBLISHING
ISSUES
AUTHORS
DEAL WITH

B Alan Bourgeois
AWARD-WINNING AUTHOR
AWARD-WINNING BESTSELLING
AUTHOR ADVOCATE

LEARN HOW TO
AVOID THE
MISTAKES

Are you an aspiring author struggling with the daunting publishing process? Look no further than "Top Ten Publishing Issues Authors Deal With." This essential guide tackles the most common challenges writers face, including rejection, editing, marketing, distribution, audience building, time management, and legal issues like copyright infringement. Our expert advice will help you navigate the complex world of publishing and achieve success. Plus, we'll guide you through the formatting process, even for ebooks that need to work on multiple devices and software. Don't let self-doubt and imposter syndrome hinder your progress - get the knowledge you need to thrive in the publishing world. Order your copy of "Top Ten Publishing Issues Authors Deal With" today.

B Alan Bourgeois

Top Ten Marketing Materials an Author Should Use

"Top Ten Marketing Items Authors Should Use" is the ultimate guide for authors who want to boost book sales and increase visibility. Discover the top ten marketing materials every author should use, including eye-catching bookmarks, business cards, posters, and book trailers. You'll also learn insider tips on how to write an attention-grabbing press release and build an author website that attracts readers and media attention. Plus, social media marketing, author blogging, email newsletters, and swag creation strategies will help you connect with readers, build your author brand, and create a loyal fan base. Don't let your book languish in obscurity - get your copy of "Top Ten Marketing Items Authors Should Use" today and take the first step towards successful book promotion!

Top Ten Mistakes an Author Makes Marketing Their Books

Are you an author struggling to make a name for yourself in the crowded world of book marketing? Do you want to avoid the most common mistakes that authors make when promoting their books? Then look no further than "Top 10 Mistakes Authors Make Marketing Their Books" by B Alan Bourgeois.

As an award-winning author and author advocate with years of experience in the publishing industry, Bourgeois has seen it all when it comes to book marketing. In this insightful guide, he shares the top 10 mistakes that authors make and provides practical advice on how to avoid them.

Whether you're a first-time author or a seasoned pro, "Top 10 Mistakes Authors Make Marketing Their Books" is the essential guide for taking your book marketing to the next level. With Bourgeois's expert guidance, you'll learn how to identify your target audience, build a strong online presence, engage with readers, and leverage book reviews to increase sales.

Don't let common marketing mistakes hold you back from the success you deserve. Get your copy of "Top 10 Mistakes Authors Make Marketing Their Books" today and start marketing your book like a pro!

B Alan Bourgeois

Top Ten Mistakes Authors Make During an Interview

Are you tired of stumbling through interviews, leaving the audience uninterested and disengaged? Do you struggle with staying focused and concise when answering tough questions? Look no further!

Our book provides you with the top ten mistakes authors commonly make at interviews and gives you practical tips on how to avoid them. From preparing adequately by researching the interviewer and their audience, to staying authentic and avoiding complex jargon, we cover it all.

Don't let your lack of enthusiasm or defensiveness turn off your audience. Instead, learn how to show genuine interest in your topic and stay calm during challenging questions. And most importantly, don't forget to thank your interviewer and audience for their time and attention - it can make all the difference in leaving a positive impression.

So, are you ready to improve your interview skills and leave a lasting impact on your audience? Get your copy of "Top Ten Mistakes Authors Do at Interviews" today!

Top Ten Mistakes Authors Make Presenting at Events

Are you an author struggling to present at events? "Top Ten Mistakes Authors Make Presenting at Events" is here to help you avoid common pitfalls and present your best self. Learn how to tailor your presentation to the audience's needs, engage with them effectively, promote your book without being pushy, and more!

With this ultimate guide, you'll avoid going off-topic, losing your audience's attention, and being dull and uninteresting. Practice and rehearse your presentation to deliver it smoothly and confidently. Get your copy of "Top Ten Mistakes Authors Make Presenting at Events" today and make the most of every event you attend!

Top Ten AI Programs Apps Authors Should Use

Attention all writers and authors! Are you looking for ways to improve your writing, stay organized, and streamline your workflow? Look no further than our latest book "Top Ten AI programs/Apps a writer/author should use". In this book, we have compiled a list of the top ten AI programs and apps that will help you with your writing, marketing, and workflow. From Grammarly and ProWritingAid to Hemingway and Dragon Dictation, these programs will help you write a great book.

Although the author has not used all of the programs listed, this list was compiled in 2023 from various sources and provides valuable insight into the most effective AI tools for writers and authors. Keep in mind that the AI community is constantly developing new resources and programs, so this list may not be the most up-to-date.

Don't miss out on the opportunity to improve your writing and streamline your workflow. Order "Top Ten AI programs/Apps a

B Alan Bourgeois

writer/author should use" now and start using these powerful tools to produce your best work.

Top Ten Advantages Indie Authors Have Over Traditional Authors

"Top Ten Advantages Indie Authors Have over Traditional" is the ultimate guide for authors looking to take control of their publishing process. With complete control over everything from writing to distribution, independent authors have more flexibility and creative control over their work.

This book highlights the benefits of indie publishing, including higher royalties, faster publishing timelines, the ability to target niche markets, and global distribution through online retailers. If you want more control over your book's content and the ability to reach readers worldwide, "Top Ten Advantages Indie Authors Have over Traditional" is a must-read. Get your copy today and start your journey towards independent publishing success!

B Alan Bourgeois

Top Ten Pieces of Advice from an Author Advocate & Consultant

"Top Ten Pieces of Advice from an Author Advocate & Consultant" is the ultimate guide for aspiring writers. Learn from an experienced author consultant and advocate and take your writing career to the next level. From building an author platform to developing a marketing plan, this book offers invaluable insights and practical tips to help you achieve your writing goals and make your work stand out. Start your journey to becoming a successful author today by purchasing this must-have resource.

Top Twelve Things to Make the Year of the Indie Authors Great

Are you an indie author looking to make 2024 a great year for your writing career? Then look no further than the book "Top Twelve Things to Make the Year of the Indie Authors Great." This book offers valuable insights into the top 12 things that could make 2024 a great year for indie authors to gain more readers.

With increased acceptance of self-publishing and better distribution channels, indie authors have more options than ever before to reach a wider audience. Additionally, the rise of social media platforms and digital marketing offers affordable ways for authors to connect with readers and promote their work.

But that's not all. The book also covers the importance of collaborating with other authors, the increasing popularity of audiobooks, and the need for more diverse representation in literature. And for those looking to improve their writing skills and production quality, the book offers insights into the better tools and resources available to indie authors.

Finally, the book covers opportunities for indie authors to engage with their readers, showcase their work at book festivals and online events, and collaborate with traditional publishers. In short, "Top Twelve Things to Make the Year of the Indie Authors Great" is a must-read for any indie author looking to take their writing career to the next level in 2024.

B Alan Bourgeois

Top Ten Steps for a Writers Self-Care

Writing can be an exciting and fulfilling pursuit, but it can also be stressful and overwhelming. As an author, it's important to prioritize your mental and physical health to avoid burnout and ensure longevity in your career. The Writer's Self-Care Handbook provides a comprehensive guide to help you balance your work and personal life, manage stress, and prioritize your well-being.

In this book, you'll discover practical tips and strategies for taking breaks, practicing mindfulness, setting boundaries, staying organized, connecting with others, taking care of your physical health, practicing self-compassion, finding healthy ways to manage stress, taking time for hobbies, and seeking support when needed. Whether you're a seasoned author or just starting out, The Writer's Self-Care Handbook offers valuable insights and advice to help you thrive in your writing career while taking care of yourself. Take the first step towards a healthier, happier writing life by getting your copy today!

Top Ten Steps to Finding the Right Editor

Are you struggling to find the right editor for your writing project? Look no further than "The Author's Guide to Finding and Working with the Right Editor." In this comprehensive guide, we provide the top ten things authors should keep in mind when finding and working with an editor. From determining your editing needs to maintaining a positive relationship with your editor, this guide covers everything you need to know to ensure a successful collaboration. Learn how to research potential editors, check their credentials, communicate clearly, be open to feedback, and more. Whether you're a first-time author or a seasoned pro, this guide is essential for anyone looking to take their writing to the next level with the help of a skilled and trusted editor.

B Alan Bourgeois

Top Ten Ways to Brand Yourself as an Author

As an author, it's not just enough to write an amazing book. In today's crowded marketplace, building a brand is essential to stand out and make a lasting impression on readers. In "Brand Yourself as an Author," we provide a top ten guide to help you define your brand identity, create a unique logo, develop a consistent visual identity, build a professional website, use social media to promote your brand, create valuable content, leverage email marketing, collaborate with other authors and brands, participate in events and conferences, and stay true to your brand. With our actionable tips, you'll learn how to build a strong and recognizable brand that resonates with your audience and sets you apart in the competitive world of publishing. Don't miss out on this essential guide to building your author brand!

Top Ten Keys for Successful Writing and Productivity

Are you an aspiring writer struggling to make writing a regular habit? Do you need help setting realistic goals and managing your time effectively to achieve success as an author? Look no further than "The Successful Author's Guide to Writing and Productivity." This comprehensive guide offers practical tips on making writing a habit, setting achievable goals, managing your time, focusing on quality, editing and revising, seeking feedback, building an audience, networking, staying organized, and staying motivated. With advice from successful authors, editors, and writing coaches, this book is a must-have for anyone looking to achieve success as an author. Whether you're a new writer or an experienced author looking to take your writing to the next level, "The Successful Author's Guide to Writing and Productivity" will provide you with the tools and techniques you need to achieve your writing goals. Don't wait any longer to become the successful author you've always wanted to be - grab a copy of "The Successful Author's Guide to Writing and Productivity" today!

B Alan Bourgeois

Top Ten Keys to the Business of Writing

Are you an aspiring or established author struggling with the business side of publishing? Look no further than The Business of Writing: A Comprehensive Guide for Authors. This essential guide provides in-depth information on the top ten items that every author needs to understand, from publishing contracts to managing finances. Learn how to negotiate contract terms, calculate royalties, promote and market your book, build an author platform, and understand copyright laws and intellectual property. You'll also gain insights into the publishing industry, professional networking, and ongoing professional development. With practical advice and expert insights, The Business of Writing is the ultimate resource for authors who want to succeed in the competitive world of publishing.

Top Ten Steps to Research Like a Pro

Writing a book can be a daunting task, but conducting research to support your writing can be just as challenging. With "Research Like a Pro: The Ultimate Guide for Writers," you'll learn how to conduct research like a pro, from identifying your research needs to analyzing your findings.

This book provides practical tips on how to use reliable sources, develop a research plan, and organize your materials effectively. You'll learn how to take detailed notes, keep track of citations, and analyze your research to identify patterns and themes.

With "Research Like a Pro," you'll be equipped with the knowledge and tools to effectively use research to support your writing. Whether you're a new writer or a seasoned pro, this book will help you take your research skills to the next level and produce high-quality writing that is well-supported and grounded in evidence.

B Alan Bourgeois

Top Ten Steps to Market Mastery for Authors

Introducing "Top Ten Steps to Market Mastery for Authors." This comprehensive guide is the key to successfully publishing your book and achieving commercial success. It goes beyond simply writing a book and equips you with the essential knowledge and tools to understand and captivate your target market.

From conducting thorough market research to analyzing sales data, "Market Mastery" covers it all. Discover how to leverage social media effectively, connect with readers at book fairs and conferences, and gain valuable insights through writing groups. Stay ahead of industry trends and developments to keep your book relevant and appealing to your audience.

No matter if you're a first-time author or a seasoned pro, "Market Mastery" will empower you to identify your target audience, understand their preferences, and distinguish your book from competitors. With a strategic marketing approach and willingness to adapt, you'll be on the path to commercial success. Get ready to conquer your target audience and take your writing career to new heights with "Market Mastery."

Top Ten Steps to Creating an Author Platform

Are you an author looking to build your online presence and connect with your readership? Then " Top Ten Steps to Creating an Author Platform " is the perfect resource for you. With practical tips on defining your target audience, establishing a website, creating a blog, building an email list, utilizing social media, attending events and conferences, collaborating with other authors, offering free content, and being consistent, this guide has everything you need to build and maintain a strong author platform. By following the advice of successful authors and marketing experts, you'll learn how to attract readers, establish yourself as an authority in your field, and promote your work effectively. Whether you're a new or experienced author, " Top Ten Steps to Creating an Author Platform " is an essential tool for any writer looking to take their career to the next level. Don't wait any longer to build your online presence - grab a copy today and start building your author platform!

B Alan Bourgeois

Top Ten Keys to Author Networking

Are you an aspiring author struggling to make industry connections? Are you looking for ways to expand your network and take your writing career to the next level? Look no further than " Top Ten Keys to Author Networking." This comprehensive guide offers practical advice on attending conferences and events, joining writing organizations, connecting on social media, attending book signings and readings, participating in online forums, attending book fairs, joining Twitter pitch parties, reaching out to authors in your genre, and maintaining a professional and polite demeanor. With tips from successful authors and industry professionals, this book is a must-have for any writer looking to make meaningful connections in the publishing world. Don't miss out on the opportunity to expand your network and increase your chances of success - grab a copy of " Top Ten Keys to Author Networking " today!

Top Ten Reasons an Author Should Use NFT and Blockchain

Top Ten Reasons an Author Should Use NFT and Blockchain is packed with invaluable insights and practical advice, this ultimate guide empowers authors on their journey to digital publishing success. Discover compelling reasons to embrace NFTs, from ensuring authenticity and automating royalties to exploring limited editions and global accessibility. Gain essential knowledge on creating NFTs, mastering smart contracts, and navigating legal considerations. Don't miss your chance to create a lasting legacy and tap into the transformative power of NFTs and blockchain. Get your copy today and embark on a journey towards publishing success! Unlock the potential of NFTs and blockchain technology with "Top Ten Reasons an Authors Should Use NFT and Blockchain.

B Alan Bourgeois

Top Ten Steps to Build an Engaged Reader Community

Top Ten Steps to Build an Engaged Reader Community the ultimate guide for authors who want to connect with their audience and create a supportive network. Learn how to define your target audience, master social media engagement, start a captivating blog, offer exclusive content, interact with readers, host virtual events, collaborate with other authors, create a compelling newsletter, encourage user-generated content, and show appreciation. With proven strategies and practical advice, this book empowers you to cultivate a supportive and enthusiastic community around your writing, propelling your author career to new heights. Don't miss out on this transformative opportunity!

The Non-Fiction Nexus: AI and the Future of Writing

The Non-Fiction Nexus: AI
and the Future of Writing
Should AI Replace Non-Fiction Writers?
B Alan Bourgeois

Numerous enterprises have leveraged literary works spanning across eras to steer their Artificial Intelligence down the path of comprehending human existence, with a more distinct focus on crafting top-tier human-like prose. In the realm of education, AI has ingeniously generated an array of refined intellectual compositions. This leads us to ponder: "Should AI replace non-fiction writers?" "The Non-Fiction Nexus: AI and the Future of Writing" delves into both the advantageous and adverse facets of this query, shedding light on the AI perspective. The book explores the current AI landscape in writing, offering a glimpse into the present state and a tantalizing peek into the potential future.

B Alan Bourgeois

Narrative Nexus: The AI Dilemma in Fiction

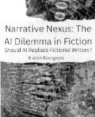

Numerous enterprises have leveraged literary works spanning across eras to steer their Artificial Intelligence down the path of comprehending human existence, with a more distinct focus on crafting top-tier human-like prose. In the realm of education, AI has ingeniously generated an array of refined intellectual compositions. This leads us to ponder: "Should AI replace fictional writers?" "Narrative Nexus: The AI Dilemma in Fiction" delves into both the advantageous and adverse facets of this query, shedding light on the AI perspective. The book explores the current AI landscape in writing, offering a glimpse into the present state and a tantalizing peek into the potential future.

Authors' Revolution Workbook

Welcome to the Speakers Companion Workbook. This workbook is a continuous transforming workbook to help Authors better understand the cost of being an Author in today's publishing world.

The author will review all the hidden cost of being a published author in todays world. In addition, he reviews a variety of companies and organizations that are available to help an author succeed.

The initial workbook in the form of an eBook is free to anyone who attends one of my speaking engagements. Updates can be purchased through my website at http://BourgeoisMedia.com .

We encourage Authors to submit information and updates to us so that we can continue to create a healthy and positive revolution that brings more financial security to each author who wants to earn their fair share from the works they have created. You may submit your comments and praise to us directly via email at BourgeoisMedia@outlook.com

B Alan Bourgeois

Milton Keynes UK
Ingram Content Group UK Ltd.
UKHW050637250923
429338UK00018B/977